11/91

ROBERT GARDNER

SCIENCE
EXPERIMENTS

ILLUSTRATIONS BY ANNE CANEVARI GREEN

FRANKLIN WATTS I 1988 I A FIRST BOOK I NEW YORK I LONDON I TORONTO I SYDNEY

Cover photograph courtesy of Bernard Asset,
Agence Vandystadt/Photo Researchers, Inc.

Library of Congress Cataloging-in-Publication Data

Gardner, Robert, 1929– Science experiments/Robert Gardner;
Illustrations by Anne Canevari Green.
    p.   cm.—(A First book)
Bibliography: p.
includes Index.
Summary: Provides instructions for science experiments and
projects in botany, physics, energy, and nature, using such everyday
objects as kitchen utensils, sink, and bathtub.
ISBN 0-531-10484-2
1. Science—Experiments—Juvenile literature. (1. Science—
Experiments. 2. Experiments.) I. Green, Anne Canevari, ill.
II. Title.
Q164.G375   1988
507'.8—dc19   87-19880 CIP AC

CONTENTS

SCIENCE EXPERIMENTS

CHAPTER ONE

TO THE READER

People become scientists because they enjoy trying to discover new things and understand how they work. Medical researchers want to know how the human body works, what causes diseases, and how diseases or disorders can be cured or treated. Inventors try to find better ways to do things, be it opening cans or traveling through outer space. Architects seek beauty and efficiency in the structures they design. Engineers try to find better and easier ways to build bridges or make chemical substances. Research scientists in all fields are searching for a better understanding of some piece of the universe. Their search may involve an attempt to probe the tiny particles that make up the basic structure of matter or to understand strange light or radio waves coming from the outer edges of space. But all scientists share common feelings: the thrill of discovery and the desire to learn more about our world.

You may find some area of science so interesting and exciting that you want to make it your life's work. But even lawyers, plumbers, factory workers, and people in all kinds of other jobs can still enjoy science. After all, people who are not professional athletes play tennis, baseball, basketball, or football simply because they enjoy it. Similarly, many people enjoy keeping weather records, collecting butterflies, watching birds, or growing plants. So whether or not you will use science in your work, you can still find pleasure in science activities both now and later in life.

Many of the major issues that do and will receive national and worldwide attention involve science. Problems raised by air pollution, acid rain, shrinking energy sources, and many other important issues can be studied and intelligently discussed only by people who have a sound grasp of science. So you see that an understanding of science and the way scientists work are important to you whether you become a scientist or not.

Doing the experiments and activities in this book will give you a better grasp of what science is. But there is no need to feel that you have to do all the experiments. Choose those that interest you most. A few require that you do another experiment first, but most can be done in any order. As you get into doing science, you may find that some of the experiments you passed over now seem more interesting. You may want to go back and do them. You may also discover new questions as you experiment. These questions may lead you to design and conduct experiments of your own.

Whether the experiments you are doing are your own or those found in this book, you should try to proceed in a scientific manner. Think about what you are going to do before you begin. Carefully observe what happens in the course of the experiment and record your observations and any measurements you make in a notebook. Did the experiment confirm what you thought would happen, or were you surprised by the results? If you were surprised, can you now explain what happened?

If the experiment raises new questions you can't explain, try to design experiments that will help you answer those questions. Don't be afraid to discuss questions, experiments, and confusing results with others. That's what most scientists do. **Before you proceed with experiments of your own design, have a knowledgeable adult check them to be sure they are safe.**

In fact, before you start experimenting, there are some things you should remember for the safety of yourself and others.

1. Be careful! Before you carry out an experiment that you have developed by yourself, check with an adult to be sure it is safe. If it involves the use of fire, glassware, or anything that could be dangerous, ask a parent, teacher, or another responsible adult to help you. Don't run the risk of injuring yourself or others. If the title of an experiment described in this book is preceded by a H, you should get an adult to help you. Sometimes, only part of the experiment needs supervision.

2. Never mix chemicals without specific instructions. Never touch chemicals with your bare hands.

3. Do not fool around while experimenting. You can enjoy science and still be serious about it.

4. Do not experiment with household electricity. You could get a dangerous electrical shock.

5. Clean up after you finish an experiment. Thoughtful scientists do not let their work interfere with what others are doing.

6. If you are doing an experiment that takes a long time, set it up in an out-of-the-way place.

CHAPTER TWO

SUMMER SCIENCE IN THE SUN

Science is fun any time of the year. But in summer you can see things and do experiments that can't be done any other season. The experiments that follow are ones that are best done in the summer when the weather is warm and the sun is high in the sky.

WATCHING WILDFLOWERS GROW

In the summer, open fields are often filled with colorful wild-flowers which add to the beauty of a summer day. If you watch the wildflowers in a field through the summer, you may observe some interesting changes. You could start your observations in March, April, or May, when wildflowers begin to bloom in the field. Make your observations near the first and fifteenth of each month until the flowers disappear in autumn's cold.

How many different kinds of flowers do you see? Can you

identify them? Do the flowers that bloom first continue to flower all summer? Or are they replaced by later flowers?

Measure the height, from ground to blossom, of at least five plants of each type. Then find the average height for each type of plant you measured. Make a graph of the average height for each of the dates on which you make measurements. Use colored construction paper to make a strip 1 inch (2.5 cm) wide. The length of the paper strip should be the same as the average height of the flowers you measured. Then tape or paste the strip to a large sheet of cardboard. Each month make another strip and tape it next to the previous one.

Do you see any changes in the average height of the wildflowers as summer progresses? Try to think of an explanation for any changes you observe.

MAKING SEEDS GROW

If you plant a garden in the spring, you'll have fresh vegetables through much of the summer. What do the seeds you plant need in order to germinate and grow? Do they require light? moisture? soil? air?

To find out how water affects germination, place a few corn, bean, or radish seeds in a dry container. In a second container place some seeds on a moist paper towel. Check it twice a day to be sure the towel is moist (not wet). Place some other seeds in a third container. Fill this container with water so the seeds are submerged. Cover all three containers.

Watch these seeds for a few days. Which ones germinate? Which do not? What conditions do you conclude are necessary for seeds to germinate?

Design an experiment to help you decide if seeds need light to sprout. Try it. What do you find? Design and carry out an experiment to determine how germination is affected by temperature.

DO PLANTS "LIKE" LIGHT?

You may have discovered that some seeds will germinate in darkness. But how long will they continue to grow in darkness?

To find out, plant some bean or corn seeds in some soil or vermiculite in two identical containers. Place one container in a dark place. Put the other one in a well-lighted area. Keep the soil in both containers moist (not wet) as the seeds germinate and grow. Observe the plants growing in both places for several weeks. What differences, if any, do you notice between the two sets of plants?

Young plants that have just germinated and begun to grow are called seedlings. Do seedlings need light to grow? Will plants grown in darkness continue to grow to maturity?

What happens if you take plants growing in darkness and place them in light? How about the reverse? Take plants growing in light and put them in darkness. What happens to them?

Find out what happens if just one leaf of a plant is covered so that it receives no light. Find out whether plants are affected by the color of the light in which they grow.

UPSIDE-DOWN PLANTS

Can plants tell up from down? To find out, take some seedlings growing in a container and turn the container on its side as shown in Figure 1. Observe these plants for a few days. Do the plants now grow sideways or do they turn and grow upward?

Modify this experiment to find out what happens if the growing plants are turned so that they are upside down.

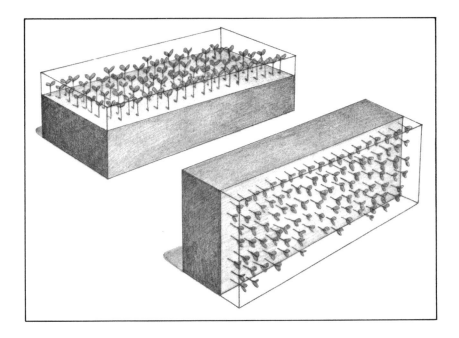

Figure 1. Growing seeds in a container

SPINNING SEEDLINGS

When you go around in a circle on a bicycle, you lean inward. Would plants grow differently if they moved in a circle as they grew? To find out, you can watch some seedlings growing on an old, spinning turntable that was once used to play records.

Plant some corn or grass seeds in some soil or vermiculite in a long, narrow plastic container. The length of the container should be about the same as the diameter of the turntable. When the seedlings begin to break through the soil, fasten the container to the turntable. Start the turntable spinning and watch the seedlings for a few days as they grow.

To see how speed affects their growth, compare the seedlings near the center of the turntable with those near the outside. Which plants are moving fastest? slowest? What do you conclude about the effect of speed on the growth of the plants?

Do you think the rate at which the turntable spins will affect the growth of the plants? Will the growth pattern change if the turntable stops spinning after the plants have grown several inches (centimeters)? What happens if you wait until the plants are several inches (centimeters) tall before you start the turntable? Explain your observations.

HIBERNATING FROGS

During the summer you can find frogs and other animals in swamps and ponds, but as winter approaches many pond animals, including frogs, disappear. Unlike a human, a frog does not have a fixed body temperature. In the winter both its body temperature and heart rate drop. The frog goes into a deep "sleep" called hibernation. However, a frog must keep its body above freezing so it burrows into the mud and leaves at the bottom of the pond. There, beneath the cold water and ice, a frog spends the winter.

If you can catch a frog, you can watch what happens as the temperature drops. Cover the bottom of a large jar with about 3 or 4 inches (8 or 10 cm) of gravel and leaves. Then fill the jar very nearly to the top with water from the pond where you caught the frog. Put the frog into the water along with a thermometer. Record the temperature and the frog's pulse rate. You can measure its pulse by watching its throat move. Count the number of times the frog's throat moves in one minute.

Now cool the water around the frog by placing the large jar in a pan of ice. Record both the temperature and the frog's pulse as the water cools. What happens to the frog's pulse as the water gets colder?

Does the frog move to the bottom of the jar? Does it try to push its way into the gravel on the bottom?

Be sure to record the temperature when the frog stops moving. At this point, don't let the temperature get any lower. Take the jar out of the ice and place it in a warm room. Continue to watch and record the temperature of the water as it warms. Also record the frog's pulse rate. How warm is the water when the frog begins to move about? What happens to the frog's pulse rate as the water approaches room temperature? How long does it take before the frog is its "old self" again?

After the experiment, be sure to return the frog to the place where you found it.

Try to visit the pond where you caught the frog during the late summer and fall. Watch the frogs and other animals in their natural habitat. Which animals hibernate? When do they begin to hibernate?

THE COLORS IN LEAVES

When summer days shorten and the nights grow cooler, leaves in many parts of the country take on brilliant colors of red, orange, and yellow that glisten in the sunlight of late summer or early fall. Do these colors develop in early autumn or are they always present?

To find out, gather a few green leaves from trees such as maples that produce bright fall colors. (Avoid poisonous leaves such as poison ivy and sumac.)

To separate the colors in the leaf you will need some strips of filter paper or white blotter paper, rubbing alcohol, and a tall cylinder or beaker. **Be careful when working with alcohol. It is flammable.**

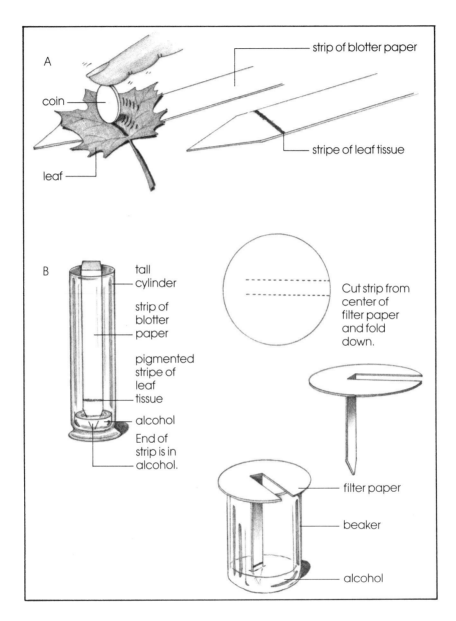

Figure 2. Exploring the colors in leaves

Place a leaf on the paper, near one end as shown in Figure 2A. Roll the edge of a coin or washer over the leaf to crush the leaf tissue and transfer the green color onto the paper. Repeat this several times using a fresh part of the leaf each time. Prepare at least one strip like this for each type of leaf you collected. After the green leaf material on the paper has dried, place the strips of blotter paper or filter paper in tall cylinders or beakers as shown in Figure 2B.

Watch the alcohol carry the green color up the paper. This will take a few minutes, but if you cover the beaker or cylinder with a dish or glass plate, the alcohol will move faster. Does a green leaf contain other colors? Experiment with different kinds of leaves to see what colors are hidden in them.

Some people think that the amount of light a tree receives affects its fall colors. Look for a maple tree located near a street lamp. Determine whether the extra light it receives affects its colors or the time it takes for these colors to develop. Compare the tree with similar trees that do not receive this extra light. What do you find?

PRESERVING LEAVES

You can preserve beautiful autumn leaves by drying them in warm, dry sand. Place a smooth layer of sand over the bottom of a metal pan. Carefully spread as many colored leaves as will fit on the sand. Cover the leaves with another layer of sand. Then place the pan about 8 inches (20 cm) above a 60-watt light bulb so that the sand will stay warm for several days. You can use concrete blocks or bricks to support the pan above the light bulb. After a few days, remove the leaves and store them in clear plastic bags.

When you listen to the howling winter wind, a glance at these beautiful leaves will remind you of warm autumn days.

STAYING COOL

How can you stay cool on an uncomfortably hot summer day? One way is to stand in front of a fan. The moving air makes you feel cooler, but is moving air cooler than still air?

To find out, read a thermometer that is at rest in still air. Then turn on a fan. Hold the thermometer in front of the fan. If you don't have a fan, use a newspaper to move air over the thermometer. You will find that the moving air is no cooler than air at rest.

Since moving air has the same temperature as still air, why does a fan make you feel cooler? To find out, spread some lukewarm water on the palm of one of your hands. Leave the other hand dry. Swing both palms through the air swiftly to create a breeze over your hands. Which palm feels cooler?

Eventually, your palm becomes dry. Water has evaporated from your skin. This means the water has become a gas (water vapor). Apparently, evaporation can make things cool. When you sweat, the heat required to make the perspiration evaporate comes from your body. This makes you feel cooler. If you have been swimming and stand in a breeze, you may begin to shiver even on a hot day because moving air makes the liquid evaporate faster.

Design experiments to find out how each of the following affects how fast a liquid evaporates:

The kind of liquid (for example, water and alcohol). **But remember, alcohol is flammable.**

The temperature of the liquid.

The amount of wind.

The humidity (moisture content) of the air.

The quantity of liquid evaporating.

The amount of surface exposed to the air.

Test just one factor at a time. If you are investigating the effect of temperature on evaporation, other factors such as wind, surface, humidity, and the kind of liquid should be the same. Only the temperature should change.

A SWINGING SWING PENDULUM

You've probably seen a grandfather clock. It has a long pendulum that swings back and forth at a steady rate. A playground swing in your yard or park is like a pendulum. It too swings back and forth at a constant rate.

The time it takes a pendulum to make one full swing, over and back, is called the period of the pendulum. To find the period of a swing, have someone sit on the swing. Give the person a push. Then measure the time it takes for that person to make ten complete swings. Divide the time by ten and you will have the period of your swing pendulum. Why is it more accurate to time ten swings rather than one?

Try the same experiment with a much heavier person. Is the period the same or different? How about a much lighter person?

Give a harder push to see if the distance through which the person swings affects the period. Measure the period of swings that have very different lengths. Does the length of a pendulum affect its period?

Watch people and animals as they walk. See how fast the short legs of a small dog move as it walks. Now watch the movement of a tall dog's legs as it walks. Compare the period of a professional basketball player's legs with the period of a small child's legs. Do legs behave like pendulums?

SUN AND SHADOWS

During summer months, your shadow is often by your side for many hours. But have you ever looked closely at your shadow and the shadows of other things?

What happens to the length of your shadow from sunrise to sunset? What happens to the direction along which your shadow lies as the day progresses?

Look at the shadow of a vertical stick or post. How does the direction of its shadow compare with yours? Does the length of a shadow depend on the height of the object that casts it?

To see how shadows change from season to season, drive a nail (be careful!) into a board or a sheet of plywood about 1 foot (30 cm) on a side. The nail should be near the center of one side of the board and about 2 inches (5 cm) in from the edge. Cut a small slit in one side of a sheet of paper. The slit will allow you to slide the paper onto the board with the nail inside the paper's perimeter as shown in Figure 3.

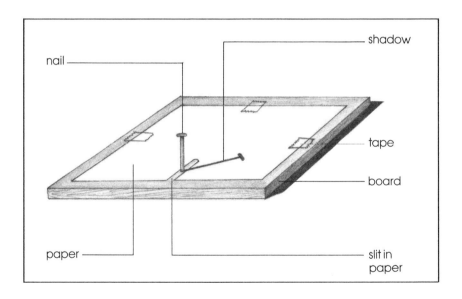

Figure 3. A simple device for tracking the seasonal changes in shadows

Put the board in a flat place where it will be in the sun all day. The side closest to the nail should be on the south side of the board. Starting early in the morning, mark the shadow of the nail on the paper every hour or two until sunset. What happens to the direction and length of the shadow as the day progresses?

Repeat the experiment at various times of the year. The beginning of each season—about the twentieth of March, June, September, and December—are good times to mark the nail's changing shadow. How does the pattern of the shadows change from season to season? Explain why the shadows change as they do.

Carefully observe other shadows that you see. They can be the source of a variety of questions that you can answer with experiments of your own.

A HAND IN SUNLIGHT

Have you ever looked closely at the shadow you cast in sunlight? By drawing the shadow of your hand on a sheet of paper taped to a piece of cardboard you can see if the size of your shadow changes with distance. Hold the paper perpendicular to the sunlight. Place your left hand above the paper (if you are right-handed) and draw the outline of the shadow of your hand on the paper. Now have someone hold the paper as you slowly move your hand away from the paper. Does your shadow get larger? smaller? Does it change in any way?

Repeat this experiment inside at night. Use a light bulb to cast shadows instead of the sun. Does the shadow of your hand change its size as you move your hand farther from, or closer to, the paper? Explain why the shadow size changes when it is cast by a light bulb, but not when it is cast by sunlight.

⊞ PINHOLE IMAGES OF THE SUN

Look at the bright patches of light beneath a leafy tree on a bright summer's day. If you look closely, you will see that these patches of light have a round shape. They are images of the sun made when sunlight shines through the small openings between the leaves.

To see how this happens, make a pinhole in an index card. Hold the card so that sunlight strikes the pinhole. Have someone hold a sheet of white paper beneath the pinhole. You will see an image of the sun on the paper. Notice how the size of the image changes as you move the paper closer to, and farther from, the pinhole.

To understand how this image is formed, **ask an adult to help you with this after-dark experiment.** Hold a pinhole punched through a sheet of dark construction paper near a burning candle in an otherwise dark room. Have someone hold a white sheet of paper taped to cardboard on the other side of the pinhole. You will see an upside-down image of the candle flame as shown in Figure 4. If you move the screen farther from the pinhole, does the size of the image change? What happens if you move the screen closer to the pinhole? What happens if you enlarge the pinhole? if you make a second pinhole? a third?

Use what you have learned to make a pinhole camera that will take pictures of nonmoving objects.

A STRANGE REFLECTION

Use a small mirror to reflect sunlight. If you hold a sheet of paper near the mirror, the reflected beam will have the shape of the mirror. But what happens as you reflect light from the mirror to greater distances? What is the shape of the beam when it falls on a wall 100 feet (30 m) or more from the mirror? Try to explain the shape of this reflected beam. Could

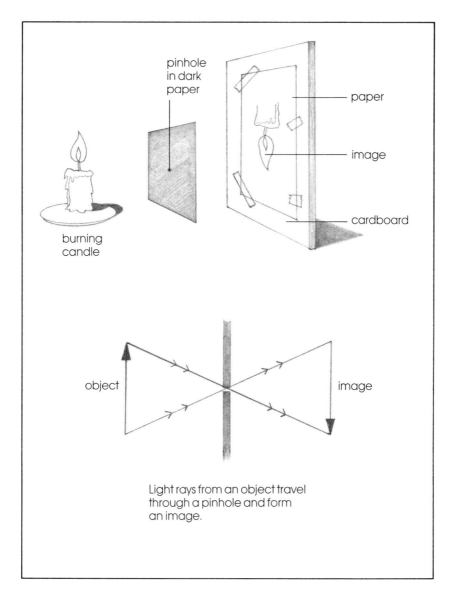

pinhole
in dark
paper

paper

image

cardboard

burning
candle

object

image

Light rays from an object travel
through a pinhole and form
an image.

Figure 4. Experimenting with pinhole images

it be related to the pinhole effect? If you think not, try the following experiment.

Make a square pinhole by folding an index card in half. Then cut a tiny half-square (a rectangle) from the center of the fold. When you open the card, you'll have a square pinhole. Let sunlight pass through the square pinhole and fall on a white sheet of paper. What happens to the shape of the light on the paper as you move the sheet farther from the pinhole?

RAINBOWS FROM A GARDEN HOSE

When did you last see a rainbow? Do you remember that the sun was behind you as you looked at the rainbow? Light was reflected from falling raindrops to your eyes.

With this principle in mind, create your own rainbow using a garden hose. Have someone spray a fine mist of water into the air while you look for the rainbow. Try to make a double rainbow. Find other ways to make rainbows. Have you tried soap bubbles?

CHAPTER THREE

WINTER SCIENCE
INSIDE AND OUTSIDE

Though snow may cover the ground and the temperature is below freezing, a lot of science can be done in your cold yard or the park or in your warm home. In fact, most of the experiments described in this chapter can be done only in the winter.

MELTING SNOW

Measure the temperature of the snow in your yard. Do this at different times of the day. Does the temperature of the snow change?

Collect a sample of snow in a container and bring it into your kitchen. Bury most of a thermometer in the snow and watch the temperature as the snow melts. When the snow melts into a slush, stir it with the thermometer. Be sure the bulb of the thermometer is submerged in the snow–water mixture. What is the temperature of melting snow? Will a larger sample of snow melt at the same or a different temperature? Fill a picnic cooler with snow and bring it inside. At what temperature does this large amount of snow melt?

How does the temperature of melting snow compare with the temperature of melting chips of chopped ice?

MELTING SNOW WITH A LENS OR WITH COAL

On a bright, sunny winter day, collect two small samples of snow from your yard. Put the two samples side by side in identical containers in a sunny place. Then use a hand lens to focus sunlight onto one of the snow samples as shown in Figure 5. Compare the time it takes to melt the snow on which

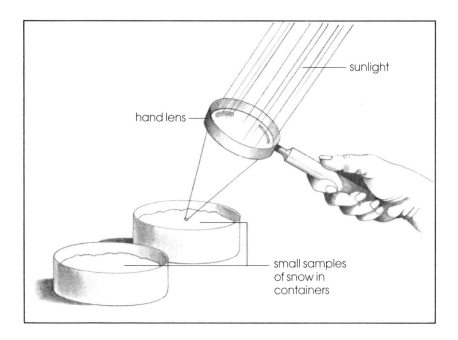

Figure 5. Melting snow with a hand lens

you focus sunlight with the time needed to melt the other sample.

Obtain two more small samples of snow in identical containers. Place both in the same sunny place. This time sprinkle a little coal or charcoal dust, or some dark dirt on one of the samples. Does the dark powder have any effect on the time required for the snow to melt?

SOLAR HEAT AND COLOR

Does the color of a material affect its ability to change sunlight into heat? To find out, obtain some identical flat pieces of metal. Squares about 2 to 3 inches (5 to 8 cm) on a side are good. Paint these metal pieces different colors—white, black, and any other colors you can find. Place the pieces of metal side by side on a snowbank that faces the sun. Which metal sinks into the snow fastest as it melts the snow beneath it? Which color changes sunlight to heat the best?

Another way to do this experiment is to cover the bulbs of identical thermometers with small pieces of different-colored construction paper (black, white, red, green, blue, etc.). A 2-inch-by-4-inch (5-cm-by-10-cm) rectangle of colored paper can be folded around the bulb of a thermometer. A paper clip or a small piece of tape can be used to hold the paper in place. Put the thermometers side by side in a sunny location. Record the temperature inside each different-colored sheet at five-minute intervals. Does color affect the change of sunlight to heat?

A MODEL SOLAR COLLECTOR

You've probably seen houses with solar collectors on roofs that face south. These panels are used to change sunlight (solar energy) into heat. The heat is used to warm air or

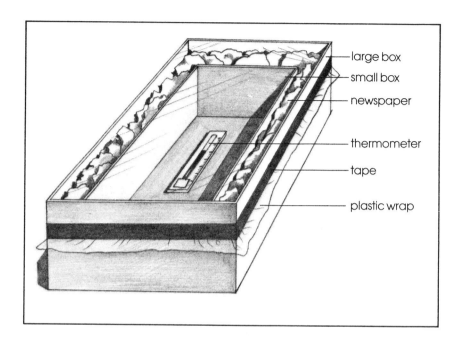

large box
small box
newspaper
thermometer
tape
plastic wrap

Figure 6. A small homemade solar collector

water. In most cases, the homeowner uses solar energy to make hot water.

You can make a small model solar collector in the following way. Find two cardboard boxes. One should be about 12 inches (30 cm) on a side. The second should be larger, about 18 inches (45 cm) on a side. Seal all seams on all but one side of the boxes with tape. Place the small box inside the larger one as shown in Figure 6. Put crumpled newspapers between the boxes. The paper will serve as insulation.

Spray the inside of the smaller box with flat black paint. Once the paint has dried, put a thermometer inside this box. Cover the bulb of the thermometer with a small piece of paper so it will not be in direct sunlight. Next, tape a sheet of clear plastic wrap over the top of the smaller box. Be sure the tape holds the plastic wrap firmly so that no air can leak around the edges. Finally, cover the top of the larger box with clear plastic, too.

Put the box in a sunny place. A thermometer that has its bulb covered with a small piece of paper can be placed beside your solar collector. Watch the temperature both inside and outside the box. What do you find?

Use different materials to build other collectors that are (a) uninsulated, (b) not painted with black paint, or (c) covered by only one layer of clear plastic wrap. How do these collectors compare with your original? Do they get as warm? Do they get warm as fast?

See if you can build a practical solar collector, one that could be used to provide hot water for washing clothes or for bathing.

ANIMAL TRACKS IN THE SNOW

If animals move about outside your house, you will be able to see the tracks they leave, particularly in wet snow. A photograph or a careful drawing of the tracks might help you identify unfamiliar animals. You can compare your drawings or photos with those in a reference book that shows the tracks of various kinds of animals. What are the most common animal tracks around your house? in a nearby field? in a forest or woods?

GET A CHARGE

During the winter, particularly on dry days, you may get an electric shock when you reach for a metal door or a doorknob after walking across a rug. This happens because the friction between your feet and the rug causes electric charges to collect on your body. When you reach for a doorknob, the charge "jumps" from your finger to the metal or to another person's body when you try to touch someone. On humid summer days, charges leak away so fast it's difficult to charge anything by rubbing.

To see how objects can be charged by rubbing, rub an inflated balloon on your clothing or against your hair. Then hold the balloon against a wall or ceiling. Charges on the balloon will attract opposite charges in the wall or ceiling. If it is a cool, dry day, the attraction of opposite charges may be enough to hold the balloon and prevent it from falling to the floor.

On a dry winter day you also can charge combs, plastic rulers, or glass or hard rubber rods by rubbing such objects with a cloth. To see that the rubbed object is charged, hold it near some small bits of paper, thread, or aluminum foil. Notice how the charge attracts these small pieces of matter. Can you make a piece of thread stand on end using the object you have charged?

With paper and scissors you can make some tiny cutout racing cars. Then you and your friends can race the cars by pulling them along with objects you have charged by rubbing them with a cloth. Try different types of cloth to see which one produces the most charge.

You can cut out tiny paper "dancers" and place them on an aluminum pie pan. Cover the pan with a sheet of plastic wrap or a clear bag. Then rub the cover with a cloth and watch the dancers move about the "ballroom."

Even water will respond to charge. To see this for yourself, hold a charged comb near a fine stream of water falling from a faucet. Notice how the water is attracted to the charged object.

To see another example of the attraction between water and a charged object, try the following. Cut a strand of steel wool into very tiny pieces. **Be careful not to get pieces of the steel in your skin**. Then charge a plastic knitting needle by rubbing it with a cloth. When you bring the tip of the needle near the pieces of steel, you will see them "leap" at the needle. Next, put a tiny piece of the steel wool on the surface of some clean water in a clear glass. Recharge the knitting needle and slowly bring its tip near the piece of metal "floating" on water. Can you explain why the metal now moves away from the same charge that attracted it before?

If not, watch the surface of the water very closely as you bring the tip of the charged knitting needle nearby. See how the water is attracted to the charge forming a small mound of water that will act as a slide for the metal.

Can you get a spark to jump from the needle to the water? (A dark room will enable you to see any such spark more easily.)

TWO KINDS OF CHARGE

Charges may repel as well as attract. To see how charges may first attract and then repel, use a small drop of glue to fasten a long piece of fine thread to a piece of aluminum foil ¼ inch (6 mm) square. When the glue has dried, tape the end of the thread to the top of a doorway so that the small piece of aluminum hangs in air. Bring a plastic (polyethylene) ruler that you have rubbed with a cloth near the aluminum. You will see it attract the aluminum, but then, as charges collect on the tiny piece of metal, the aluminum will move away from the ruler. Charges have moved from the ruler to the aluminum. The aluminum and ruler now carry the same kind of charge so they repel.

Bring a glass test tube or unconnected light bulb that has been rubbed with a cloth near a piece of aluminum that is repelled by a plastic ruler. Notice how the glass attracts the tiny piece of metal. **Be careful when handling glass**.

To find out how charged plastic rulers and glass tubes or light bulbs affect one another, make a sling from a piece of strong, plastic-covered wire. Suspend the sling from a high place using a piece of thread and some tape. Then put a plastic ruler that you have rubbed with a cloth into the sling.

What happens when you bring another ruler that has been charged in the same way near the ruler that is in the sling? Will a charged glass light bulb or test tube also repel the ruler, or do these two objects attract? What happens when you place a charged glass test tube or light bulb in the sling and bring another charged glass object near it? What happens if a charged plastic ruler is brought near the glass in the sling?

As you can see, there appear to be two kinds of charges —one kind (positive charge) is found on rubbed glass, the other (negative charge) on rubbed plastic (polyethylene). Charges of the same type (positive and positive or negative and negative) repel, but unlike charges (positive and negative) attract.

A CHARGE SHIELD

You can shield an object from electrical forces by surrounding it with metal. To see that this is true, glue a small piece of aluminum foil to a long, thin thread and hang the metal in an open doorway. Charge the metal with a plastic ruler. Notice how the foil is attracted or repelled when a charged ruler or glass tube is brought near it. Next, carefully place a large tin can, open at both ends, under the piece of aluminum. Raise the can until the foil lies at its very center. Be careful to keep the foil near the center of the can so that it does not swing to one side, touch the can and lose its charge.

With the charged foil at the center of the can, have someone bring a charged ruler or glass bulb near the outside of the can. Does the metal foil respond to the charge outside the can?

Carefully lower the can. What happens when the charged object is held the same distance from the foil without the metal can to shield it?

CONDUCTORS AND NONCONDUCTORS OF ELECTRICITY

Substances through which electric charges can move are called conductors. Nonconductors are substances through which charges do not move. To find out whether something is a conductor or a nonconductor you will need to build a battery like the one shown in Figure 7A. You can connect the battery to a flashlight bulb and leave a gap between the wires as seen in Figure 7B. To find out which solids are conductors, hold the end of the wire coming from the battery against one end of the solid being tested. Touch the end of the wire from the bulb to the other end of the solid for a short time. If the bulb lights, the solid is a conductor.

You can test a variety of solids. You might try nails, chalk, plastic and metal knitting needles, erasers, wood, paper and paper clips, silverware, glassware, pencils and pencil lead, and a variety of other solids. Which solids are conductors? Which are nonconductors or very poor conductors?

Are any liquids conductors of electricity? To find out, dip the ends of the same wires you were touching to solids into liquid in a small cup or vial. Test such liquids as water, milk, lemon juice, various fruit juices, vinegar, and solutions of baking soda, tooth powder, salt, or sugar. Solutions are made by dissolving such things as salt and sugar in water.

Repeat the experiment for the liquids that appeared to be nonconductors. Keep the wires in these liquids for several minutes. Even if the bulb doesn't light, you may find gas bubbles collecting on the wires. This indicates that a charge is being conducted even though it's not enough to make the bulb light.

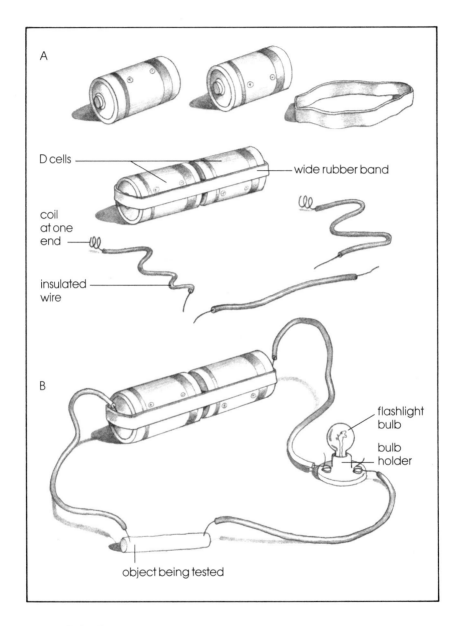

A

D cells — wide rubber band

coil at one end

insulated wire

B

flashlight bulb

bulb holder

object being tested

Figure 7. Testing for conductivity

Which liquids are good conductors? Which are nonconductors? Which are poor conductors?

Cool some solids or liquids that are good conductors by placing them in the refrigerator. Does cooling the substances change their ability to conduct electricity?

Will liquid conductors still conduct electricity if they are frozen? To find out, place a small amount of a saltwater solution in a vial. Put the vial in a freezer or outdoors if it is cold. After the liquid has frozen, test it to see if it still conducts electricity. What do you find?

CHAPTER FOUR

SCIENCE IN THE KITCHEN AND THE BASEMENT

In many ways a kitchen is an excellent laboratory. It has a stove to heat things, a refrigerator to cool or freeze substances, a sink with hot and cold water, various pans and glassware, and counters on which to set up experiments. Basements, garages, or workshops are often places where you can find the tools you need to cut wires or boards or find tacks, nails, washers, hammers, screwdrivers, and the various other tools you can use for your experiments. You'll find both the kitchen and basement good places to do science.

WATER AND LIFE

Water is essential for life. It accounts for three-quarters of your weight and is the main ingredient of the millions of cells that make up your body. Every time you exhale, some water, in the form of vapor, leaves your body. To prove that there is water in the air you breathe out, hold your mouth and nose near a cold window pane or mirror and breathe onto the cold surface. The moisture that condenses there reveals the water in the air you exhale.

Water escapes from plants, too. You can "capture" this water vapor quite easily. Use a plastic bag to cover a leafy, potted plant and a tie band to close the bag securely around the plant's stem. In this way you can be sure that any moisture you see does not come from the damp soil. Then cover the entire plant and pot with another large, clear plastic bag. Watch the plant for a day or two. What evidence do you have that plants "exhale" moisture?

As further evidence for the presence of water in living matter, weigh some food samples such as bread, meat, crackers, vegetables, or fruits. After you have weighed each item, **ask an adult to help you heat these food samples** in a 150° Fahrenheit oven for several hours.

After the food samples have cooled, reweigh each one. What has happened? Explain your results.

WATER'S SKIN

Though water is a key part of all life, water itself isn't a living thing. However, it does seem to have a "skin." You can see this for yourself. Just fill a small, clean, well-rinsed container with water. Then use a fork to gently place a paper clip on the surface of the water. The water's skin can support the paper clip. Look closely! You will see that water's supporting "skin" is curved downward where stretched by the paper clip's weight.

Can you make a needle or a pin float on water?

What happens to water's skin when you add a drop of soap solution? To find out, again place a paper clip on some water. Then add the drop of soapy water. What happens?

As you have seen, water holds together very well to form a skin. But soap gets between the water particles causing the skin to break apart so it can no longer support a light object.

FUSING STREAMS

Here's another way to see how strongly water attracts water. Punch two holes in the side of an insulated coffee cup with a small nail or a toothpick. The holes should be near the bottom of the cup and about 3/16 inch (5 mm) apart from center to center.

Fill the cup with water. You'll see two streams of water emerge from the cup. Use your fingers to "squeeze" the streams together. Can you fuse the two streams into one? Can you fuse three streams into one?

LIQUID DROPS

Because water holds together so well, you might guess that drops of water would be larger than drops of soapy water. But how can you find out for sure?

It's hard to measure a single drop, but if you measure the volume of many drops and then divide, it's easy. Just count the number of drops of water needed to fill a medicine cup to the 10-milliliter (ml) line. Suppose you count 200 drops to fill a cup with water to the 10-ml line. Each drop must have a volume of 0.05 (1/20) ml because 10 ml divided by 200 drops is equal to 0.05 ml per drop.

Repeat the experiment using soapy water and other liquids. Be sure to thoroughly clean, rinse, and dry the dropper after testing each liquid. Are water drops larger than drops of soapy water? Which of the liquids tested forms the largest drops? the smallest drops?

DROP PRINTS

When you walk in snow or mud you leave footprints. When drops of liquid fall from an eyedropper onto blotting paper, paper towels, newspaper, or construction paper, they leave "drop prints." Compare the drop prints made when drops of different liquids fall from the same height. Does the kind of paper they fall on affect the pattern of the drop prints? Does the height from which the drops fall affect any of the drop prints?

Suppose the drops are moving when they start to fall. Will that affect the drop print? To find out, move your hand in a horizontal direction above the paper when you squeeze the eyedropper to release a drop.

Let the drops fall onto paper that lies on a slanted surface by placing a board under the paper. One end of the board can be in the sink, while the other end rests against the kitchen counter. Does the fall onto a slanted board affect the drop print? How?

DROPS ON DIFFERENT SURFACES

With an eyedropper, carefully place drops of water on different surfaces such as waxed paper, aluminum, glass, plastic wrap, newspaper, or formica. Look at the drops from the side. Is their shape affected by the surface they are on? See if you can predict how these same surfaces will affect the shapes of drops of other liquids such as soapy water, alcohol, and cooking oil.

Perhaps you noticed that a water drop on a smooth surface has a lenslike shape. Lenses are used in microscopes to magnify objects so that we can see them more clearly. What do you think some newsprint will look like through a drop of water. Try it. Were you right?

How will the magnification of print using a water drop compare with the magnification using soapy water or alcohol? Again, test your predictions to see if you are right.

⊞ DROP RACES

Be sure to have an adult help you place drops of water, soapy water, alcohol, and cooking oil on one side of a piece of window glass. Then lift the side where the drops have been placed as shown in Figure 8. Which drop will win the race to the bottom of the glass?

Will the results of the race be different if it is run on aluminum foil instead of glass? How about on a waxed-paper track? on plastic wrap? on wood? newspaper?

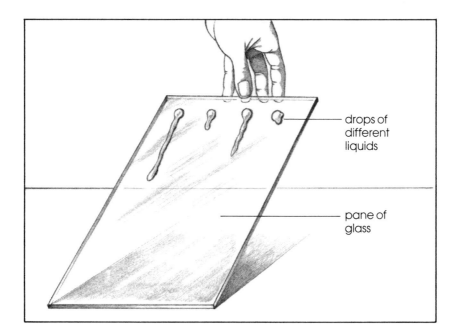

Figure 8. A liquid drop race

LIQUID PUSHES AND PULLS

Thoroughly clean and rinse a large glass dinner plate. Fill the plate with clean water. Then take a piece of lightweight thread about 12 inches (30 cm) long and tie its ends together. Place the circle of thread on the water surface. Carefully add a drop of water to the region inside the thread. Does the water push the thread outward? Next, place a drop of soapy water inside the thread. What happens this time?

To see a "war" between water and alcohol, add a drop or two of food coloring to some clean water. Spread the colored water into as thin a layer as possible across the surface of a glass plate or a formica surface. Then place a drop of rubbing alcohol in the center of the water. What happens?

Next, sprinkle a light dusting of talcum powder or chalk dust on some clean water in a large container (a cafeteria tray works well). Be sure the water is calm before you add the fine powder. From what you have seen before, try to predict what will happen when you add a drop of soapy water to the center of the powder-covered water. Were you right?

What happens if you repeat the experiment using a drop of alcohol instead of soapy water? Do you get the same effect if you spread the powder on soapy water and then add a drop of water or alcohol? Try it and see!

To see a delayed reaction between soap and water, try placing about a quarter of a teaspoonful of cooking oil on the surface of a large container of clean water. Does the oil sink or float in water? Which do you think will weigh more, a cup of water or a cup of cooking oil? If you have a balance, you can test your prediction.

After you have the cooking oil floating on the water, mix about a teaspoonful of liquid soap with 1/3 cup of water. Then carefully place one drop of this soap solution at the very center of the top of the oil blob. Predict what will happen when the soap passes through the oil and reaches the water. Will the same thing happen if you add a drop of alcohol instead of soap to the oil blob?

⊞ WATER DISSOLVED IN AIR

Just as salt and sugar dissolve in water, water dissolves in air. As you may know, more sugar will dissolve in hot water than in cold water. It's also true that more water can be dissolved in warm air than cool air. The moisture dissolved in air is called humidity. Because more water dissolves in warmer air, summer air is generally more humid (contains more moisture) than winter air.

To show that water is dissolved in air, lower the temperature until water comes out of solution; the moisture in the air will condense into liquid. To see water condense from air, add small pieces of ice to some warm water in a shiny can. Stir the water carefully with a thermometer. Watch for the temperature at which water begins to condense on the surface of the shiny can. This temperature at which moisture condenses from the air is called the dew point. Where else have you seen water condensing from air?

Use this technique to measure the dew point of air at different seasons of the year and on clear, cloudy, and humid days. What do you find?

If you have a humidifier or dehumidifier, find out how adding moisture to, or removing moisture from, the air in a room affects the dew point. First, measure the dew point in the room. Then turn on the humidifier for several hours before you measure the dew point again. How does adding moisture to the air affect the dew point? How is the dew point affected when moisture is removed from the air?

⊞ RAIN IN THE KITCHEN

You know that water dissolves in air and that warm air holds more moisture than cold air. When this warm air cools, the moisture may condense into raindrops. You can use these principles to make it "rain" in your kitchen.

Ask an adult to help you with this experiment. Hold a pan of ice over the steam coming from a teakettle of boiling water. Where do you see it "raining"?

Ⓗ FIRE EXTINGUISHER GAS

Many fire extinguishers produce a gas called carbon dioxide which can be used to put out fires. To see how this works, you can make some of this gas and then pour it onto a flame.

Ask an adult to light a birthday candle placed in a small piece of clay as shown in Figure 9. Meanwhile, cover the bottom of a wide-mouth jar, such as the kind peanut butter comes in, with a thin layer of baking soda. Pour an ounce (30

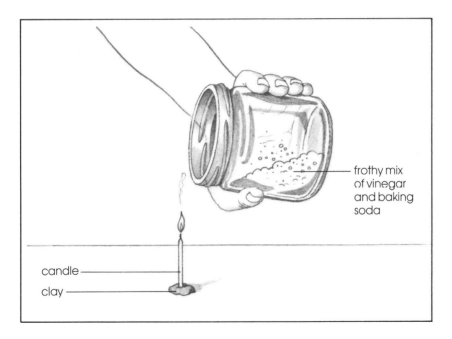

candle
clay
frothy mix of vinegar and baking soda

Figure 9. Making fire extinguisher gas

ml) of vinegar onto the baking soda. The bubbles that form are filled with carbon dioxide. Because this gas is "heavier" than air, it will soon fill the jar as it forces air upward.

After about half a minute, hold the jar over the candle and tip it so that the gas (not the vinegar) can pour out the jar and onto the flame. Why do you think the candle goes out?

MAGNETS AND NONMAGNETS

Albert Einstein (1879–1955) said it was the mysterious way in which magnets attract objects without touching them that first aroused his interest in science. Perhaps magnets will have a similar effect on you.

To begin your investigation, use a magnet to separate a variety of materials. Your collection might include some other magnets, different kinds of metal, paper, wooden and plastic articles, and some liquids. Try to separate these objects into three groups: 1) those not affected by a magnet; 2) those attracted to both ends of a magnet; and 3) those attracted by one end of the magnet and repelled by the other end.

Are all metals attracted by magnets? If not, can you find any pattern among those that are and those that aren't attracted? Are any nonmetallic materials such as wood, plastic, paper, or liquids attacted to magnets? Are any materials both attracted and repelled by a magnet? If so, what are they?

WILL MAGNETS ACT
THROUGH MATTER?

If you bring a magnet near a paper clip, pin, tack, or needle, the metal will be pulled toward the magnet. But will it be attracted if you put something between the magnet and the small piece of metal?

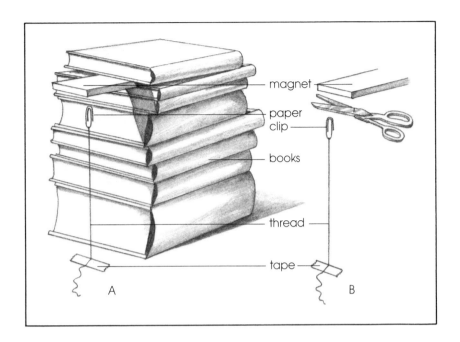

Figure 10. A "floating" paperclip

To find out, place a tack or paper clip in a glass jar. Can you move the metal within the glass jar by moving the magnet around the *outside* of the jar? Will a tack resting on a wooden ruler move if you move a magnet underneath the ruler? Will it work if the ruler is made of plastic? Conduct experiments of your own design to see if magnets act through plastic, rubber, water, metal, and paper.

If you have a reasonably strong magnet, you can make a paper clip "float" on the end of a long piece of thread as shown in Figure 10A. What do you think will happen if you slide a piece of paper or plastic between the paper clip and the magnet? Will a coin placed between the paper clip and magnet have any effect? How about a lid from a tin can? Can you "cut" the magnetic forces with a pair of scissors as shown in Figure 10B?

MAKE AN ELECTRIC METER

You can make an electric meter by wrapping about 20 yards (18 m) of thin enameled copper wire into a loop around a magnetic compass. (See Figure 11.) A piece of tape on opposite sides of the coil will hold the wires together. Use sandpaper or emery paper to remove the enamel from the two ends of the wire.

Once you have placed the wire coil around the magnetic compass, be sure that the wires in the coil are parallel to the compass needle. What happens when you connect the ends of the coil to the opposite poles of a flashlight battery? Will the meter still indicate a current if several flashlight bulbs are connected between the meter and the battery as

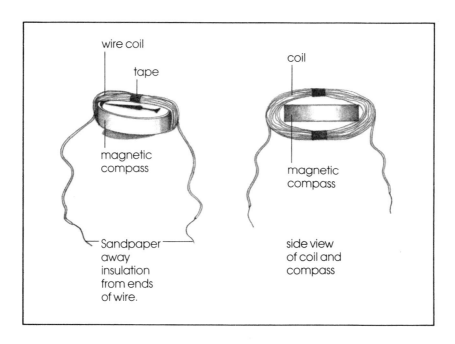

Figure 11. Making an electric meter

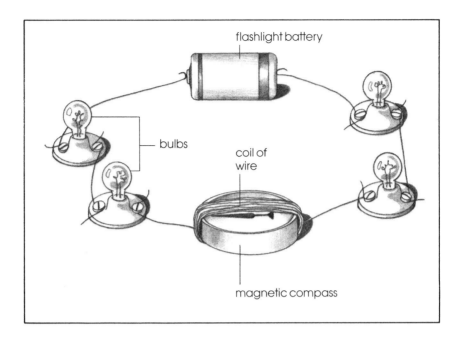

Figure 12. Using your electric meter

shown in Figure 12? Will the meter still indicate a current if there are so many bulbs in a line that none of them light?

A BATTERY YOU CAN EAT

Luigi Galvani (1737–1798) discovered that a frog's leg muscles would contract whenever touched by two different metals. Galvani thought that the electricity came from the animal tissue. Later, Alessandro Volta (1745–1827) showed that the generation of electricity did not require living tissue. He was able to produce electricity by placing two different metals in salt water.

You can duplicate Volta's discovery using metals and fruits instead of metals and salt water. If you can borrow a

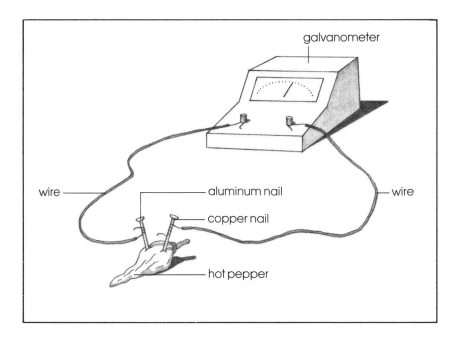

Figure 13. A hot-pepper setup that generates electricity

galvanometer or microammeter from your school, use two wires to connect the meter leads to copper and aluminum nails stuck in a small red or green pepper or an olive as shown in Figure 13. What evidence do you have that electricity is produced? Which metal is the positive electrode; that is, which metal is connected to the positive lead of the meter when the meter needle moves to the right?

If you do not have access to such a meter, you can use the meter described in the previous experiment. Support the magnetic compass with some clay and be sure the wires in the coil are parallel to the compass needle. This homemade meter is not as sensitive as a commercial galvanometer or microammeter, but it will detect small electric currents.

Figure 14 shows you the inside of a flashlight battery. You

can see that it has two electrodes—the carbon rod in its center and the zinc case that encloses the rest of the material. Between these two electrodes lies the black, damp electrolyte. An electrolyte is any material that will conduct electricity when placed in water. In your battery, the juice in the hot pepper or olive was the electrolyte. What electrolyte did Volta use?

Try other metals as electrodes for your battery. If you have an iron nail, try iron and copper as electrodes. Or use iron and aluminum electrodes. Which metal is the positive electrode in each case? You might also try strips of zinc, brass, and any other hard metals you can find. Which of these metals is always the positive electrode? Which is always the negative electrode?

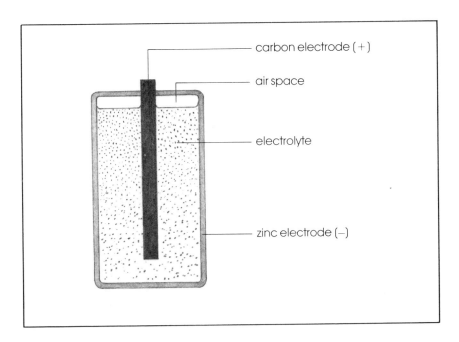

Figure 14. The parts of a D cell

You can also use other fruits as electrolytes. You might try lemons, oranges, apples, pears, and other fruits and vegetables. Which fruit or vegetable seems to be the best electrolyte? Are any of them a better electrolyte than the hot pepper or olive?

While the electrodes are connected to the meter, touch one electrode to the top of your tongue and the other to the bottom of your tongue. Does a current flow? Can you feel a weak tingling sensation?

Will a current flow if you hold the two electrodes in your hands and squeeze them with your fingers? What happens to the current if you dampen your fingers?

Does the distance between the metal electrodes when they are in the electrolyte affect the size of the electric current read on the meter? Does the depth to which the electrodes are pushed into the fruit affect the current?

SENDING A RADIO SIGNAL

When electric charges speed up or slow down, radio or television waves are produced. These waves travel to radios and television sets at the speed of light. You can produce and detect a radio signal quite easily.

Press one end of a metal wire against one end of a flashlight cell. When you briefly touch the other end of the wire to the other pole of the battery, the charge will speed up as it begins to flow through the wire. To detect the radio wave produced, turn on a small battery-operated radio and tune it to a station. Then turn the dial until the talk or music disappears and you are left with a little background static. Now send a signal with the battery and wire. Listen carefully. You will hear the signal on the radio.

If you wrap the radio in aluminum foil, will you still be able to hear the signal? Will you hear the signal if you wrap the radio in newspaper?

CHAPTER FIVE

SCIENCE IN A SINK OR A BATHTUB

Water is a key component of many experiments. Therefore, if you are a young scientist, it's nice to have a sink or bathtub for many of the experiments you'll find in this chapter. A bathtub or laundry sink is essential when experiments require deep water.

WATER UNDER PRESSURE

When the water pressure from a hose is increased, you know that water will shoot out much farther. You can use this knowledge to see how pressure changes as the depth of water increases. Use a nail to punch three identical holes in the *side* of a Styrofoam cup. Make one hole close to the bottom, one about a third of the way from the top to the bottom, and one about two-thirds of the way from top to bottom. The holes should *not* be directly above one another.

Fill the cup with water, keeping your fingers over the holes in the side. Holding the cup well above a bathtub or large sink, remove your fingers from over the holes. From which hole does the water seem to emerge with the greatest pressure? How does the depth of water in the cup affect the pressure?

Fill the bottom of the sink or tub with water before you repeat this experiment with a new twist. This time, as soon as water starts to flow from the holes, drop the cup and watch the streams carefully. If you don't believe what you saw, try it again!

Because cup and water fall at the same rate, the water stops flowing while the cup is falling.

⊞ AIR POURS UP

Turn a clear plastic tumbler upside down and lower it into a tub of water. Notice that you have trapped some air in the tumbler. Water doesn't enter the tumbler because air fills that space.

Now lower a second upside-down plastic tumbler into the tub. Turn this tumbler so that it becomes filled with water. What happens to the air in the tumbler when the tumbler is turned so that water can enter?

Now see if you can move the air trapped in the first tumbler into the second one that is filled with water. Which tumbler should be above the other? How can you get the air to move from one tumbler to the other?

⊞ A GLASS OF WATER
UPSIDE DOWN

Fill a plastic tumbler or jar brimful with water. Place a piece of a brown paper bag slightly larger than the top of the tumbler or jar on the water. Holding the paper firmly against the vessel, turn the vessel upside down over a sink or tub. When you remove your hand from the paper, air pressure will keep the water in the glass. In fact, you can place the inverted glass of water on a counter, slip the paper from beneath the glass, and challenge someone to remove the container of water from the table without spilling any.

Get an adult to help you do this experiment on a grander scale. Fill a large pail with water. Add a few drops of colored water to make the liquid more visible. Then slowly submerge a piece of clear plastic tubing about 35 feet (11 m) long in the water. Coil the tubing as you submerge it. When the entire length of tubing has been submerged, place a small cork in the end of the tubing while it is under water. Or clamp the end of the tube. Have your adult helper carry or pull the sealed end of the tube up several flights of stairs while you hold the open end submerged in the water. How tall a column of water will air pressure support?

⊞ DRINKING UPSIDE DOWN

Normally when you drink, gravity helps the liquid slide down your throat into your stomach. To see if you can drink when gravity acts against the flow of water into your stomach, **ask an adult to help you with this experiment.**

Put a straw in a glass of water that is on the floor. Place your head on a pillow resting next to the water and stand on your head. Have the adult hold your legs against a wall. Place the straw in your mouth and see if you can drink. What do you find? Do you think astronauts can drink in gravity-free space?

THE SWEET DISAPPEARING ACT

Weigh two cubes of sugar. Then weigh out an equal amount of loose (uncubed) sugar. Put the two cubes in a glass of water. Put the loose sugar in another identical glass of water. Use spoons to stir both glasses of sugar and water. In which glass does the sugar disappear (dissolve) first? Can you explain why?

How many teaspoonfuls of sugar can you dissolve in a cup of cold water if you stir the water? How many teaspoonfuls can you dissolve in a cup of warm water? How does temperature affect the amount of sugar that can be dissolved in a cup of water?

What do you think will happen if you put the warm water and its dissolved sugar in a refrigerator? Try it. Were you right?

Pour some of the cold water with its dissolved sugar into a saucer. Place the saucer in a warm place for several days. What happens? Does the sugar evaporate? How can you separate dissolved sugar from water? How could you separate the salt found in seawater?

AIR IN WATER

You've seen that more sugar will dissolve in warm water than in an equal amount of cold water. Air dissolves in water, too. After all, fish need air, or the oxygen in air, to live.

Leave a glass of cold water in a warm room for several hours. Notice the small bubbles of air that collect in the water.

Is more air dissolved in cold water or in warm water?

Why do fish often die during the summer when the water they are swimming in becomes very warm?

Carbonated beverages are made by dissolving carbon dioxide gas in flavored water. Is carbon dioxide more soluble in cold water or in warm water? To find out, open two cans of soda, one cold and the other warm. Which one produces more bubbles?

HOT WATER IN COLD WATER

When water freezes in a lake or pond, it always freezes at the surface first. Does this mean that cold water rises to the surface and is always colder than the water below? Here's a way to find out.

Fill a sink or tub with cold water. Then put a few drops of food coloring in a test tube or medicine vial. Fill the tube or vial with hot water. Seal the vessel with a cork or cover and place it on the bottom of the sink or tub of cold water. Being careful not to disturb the water, open the test tube or vial. What happens to the colored hot water when it enters the cold water?

Can you predict what will happen if you repeat the experiment with warm water in the sink and colored cold water in the small vial? Try it! Were you right?

Does this experiment explain why pond water freezes at the surface?

BALLOON LIFTS

Hot-air balloons are fun to watch. Maybe you've even taken a ride in a basket suspended from a big, colored, hot-air balloon or watched one float across the sky. If you have, you may have noticed that the pilot had to heat the air to make the balloon rise. When the air cools, the balloon descends.

You can use an ordinary balloon in a bathtub or deep sink to lift small lead sinkers or steel washers submerged in water. How many sinkers or washers can you attach to a balloon 4 inches (10 cm) in diameter before the balloon sinks? (A tie band can be used to both seal the neck of the balloon and attach weights.) Does the size of the balloon (the amount of air in it) have any effect on its lifting strength? How can you find out?

With a measuring cup you can pour hot water into the mouth of a large, empty balloon. When the balloon is completely filled, seal its neck with a tie band. (Be careful not to let air into the balloon.) The tie band can also be used to attach paper clips to the balloon. How many paper clips will a hot water balloon lift if placed in cold water? How many paper clips will the same balloon filled with cold water lift in cold water?

What do you think will happen if you place a balloon filled with cold water in a tubful of warm water? Were you right?

If you can get a helium-filled balloon, you'll see that it rises in air. Can you attach paper clips or string to the balloon so that it will stay at one place in the air, so that it neither rises nor sinks?

Fill a balloon with rubbing alcohol. What is the lifting strength of such a balloon in cold water? in warm water? How is an alcohol-filled balloon in water similar to a helium balloon in air?

CHAPTER SIX

SCIENCE UPSTAIRS, DOWNSTAIRS, AND IN A WELL-LIGHTED ROOM

Kitchens and bathrooms are not the only rooms where you can do science experiments. Some experiments can be done anywhere; some are best done in the basement; some require a stairwell in a well-lighted room; others, like the next experiment, require you to move upstairs and downstairs.

BAROMETERS: UPSTAIRS, DOWNSTAIRS, AND IN THE CAR

Scientists often use barometers containing mercury to measure the pressure of air and other gases. But because mercury is poisonous, you should use an aneroid barometer, the kind usually found in homes. It contains no mercury. The drawing in Figure 15 shows you the inside of such an aneroid barometer.

Air enters an aneroid barometer through a hole in the back. The air presses on a thin, hollow can. Most of the air

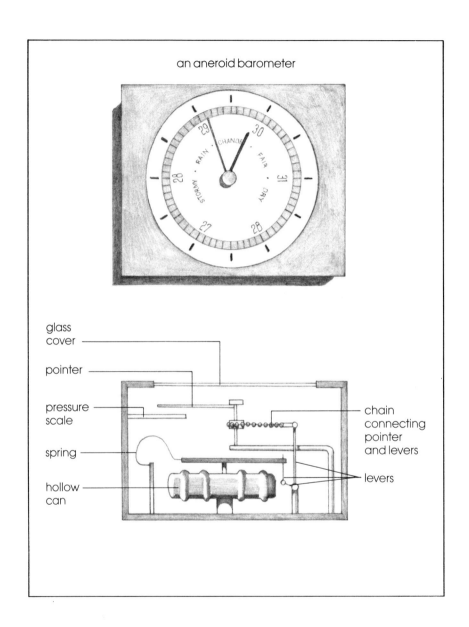

Figure 15. An aneroid barometer and its parts

was removed from the can before it was sealed so there is a good vacuum inside.

The outside of the can is connected to a spring. The end of the spring is attached, through a series of levers, to a chain that turns a pointer above a scale. When air pressure increases, the sides of the can are pushed inward. This push on the can causes the pointer to turn, indicating a higher pressure. When the air pressure decreases, the sides of the can move outward and the pointer turns in the other direction.

An aneroid barometer is smaller than a mercury barometer and can be carried easily from place to place. You can use such a barometer to test Torricelli's hypothesis.

Evangelista Torricelli (1608–1647) was an Italian scientist and mathematician. He believed that the atmosphere was a giant sea of air. Torricelli knew that as you go deeper in water the pressure increases. So he argued that as one descends into the atmosphere, the air pressure increases. Therefore, if we go up from the ground into the air, to a higher altitude, the pressure should decrease.

In 1648, Blaise Pascal (1623–1662) supervised an experiment conducted by his brother-in-law, Florin Péririer, to test Torricelli's hypothesis. A mercury barometer was carried up Le Puy de Dôme mountain in France in order to measure the air pressure at different altitudes. To see the results of Pascal's experiment, you can carry an aneroid barometer up stairs and hills.

First, make a careful reading of the air pressure in the basement or first floor of a house or apartment building. Then carry the barometer to the top floor. How does the air pressure on the top floor compare with the pressure in the basement?

If you can do it, watch the barometer as you go up and down in the elevator of a tall building.

See what happens to the air pressure as you climb a high

hill or mountain. Or, better yet, take your barometer on an auto trip. What happens to the air pressure as you go up and down high hills? If possible, take an aneroid barometer for a ride on a small airplane. What do you find?

What do you think Pérrier and Pascal concluded about Torricelli's hypothesis?

REFLECTED LIGHT

As you've seen, a barometer shows a change in air pressure when you go up or down in the earth's atmosphere. But, as nearly as we can tell, sunlight is just as bright at the top of your home or apartment as it is on the lawn or street. However, light will become less bright if it is reflected many times.

Light comes to us from the sun. We see objects in the daytime because light from the sun strikes these objects, "bounces" off them, and travels to our eyes. Reflection is the name we give to the bouncing of light from objects.

To see how light is reflected from a mirror, hold a small pocket mirror in a beam of sunlight coming through a window. With the mirror you can reflect a patch of bright light around the room. Are there any places in the room where you cannot reflect the light?

The angle made by a light beam and a mirror's surface is shown in Figure 16. Does the angle between the incoming light and the mirror seem to be related to the angle between the mirror's surface and the patch of reflected light? See what happens to the position of the bright patch as you change the angle between the light beam and the mirror.

Using the same or a different mirror, look at someone else's image in the mirror. Can that person see your image by looking in the mirror? If you increase the angle between yourself and the mirror, where must the other person stand to see your image? When you can't see the other person's image, can he or she see your image?

-60

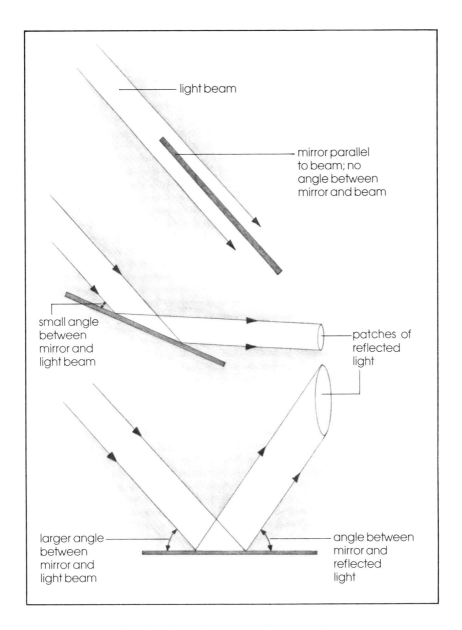

light beam

mirror parallel
to beam; no
angle between
mirror and beam

small angle
between
mirror and
light beam

patches of
reflected
light

larger angle
between
mirror and
light beam

angle between
mirror and
reflected
light

Figure 16. Investigating the effects of mirrors on light

What have you learned about reflected light from this experiment?

FINDING YOUR BEST SIDE

You may have noticed that one side of a person's face is not identical with the other side. Some people are so aware of these differences that they will only allow one side of their faces to be photographed.

To compare the two sides of your face, or someone else's, find a front-view photograph of your own or that person's face. Place the edge of an unframed mirror on the photograph so that it splits the face in half. When you look into the mirror, you will see what the person would look like if the two sides of that person's face were identical.

Now turn the mirror around and look at the image of the other side of the person's face. Is it the same face you saw when you reflected the other side of the person's face? Which side do you think is your "best" side? Do people seem to have a happy side and an unhappy side?

WHERE IS YOUR IMAGE
IN A PLANE MIRROR?

When you look into a flat mirror, you can see your image. But where is the image that you see in the mirror? One way to locate the position of an image, or any other object, is by parallax.

To see what is meant by parallax, hold a pencil at arm's length. Hold a second pencil in front of the first one, closer to your face. Notice that when you move your head first to one side and then the other, or close first one eye and then the other, the closer pencil seems to move relative to the farther pencil. This shift of one object relative to another when you change your line of sight is called parallax. Two objects always show parallax unless they are at the same place. Notice that if you place the second pencil on the first one, there will be no parallax when you change your line of sight.

You can use the principle of parallax to locate an image in a mirror. Use a piece of clay to support a small mirror as shown in Figure 17A. Another small lump of clay can be used to hold a short pencil upright in front of the mirror. Finally, use some clay to support a taller pencil behind the mirror. The top of this pencil should project above the mirror.

Line up the pencil behind the mirror with the *image* of the smaller pencil that you see in the mirror. Keep moving the taller pencil behind the mirror until there is no parallax between it and the image seen in the mirror. The taller pencil behind the mirror now "sticks" with the image of the shorter pencil seen in the mirror when you shift your head from side to side. What do you know now about the location of the image seen in the mirror?

How does the distance from the shorter pencil to the mirror compare with the distance of the pencil's image from the mirror? Repeat the experiment with the shorter pencil closer to, and farther from, the mirror. What do you find about the position of its image in each case?;

Suppose you place the shorter pencil to one side of the mirror as shown in Figure 17B. Where do you think the pencil's image is now? Again, locate the image by eliminating parallax between the image and the taller pencil. Was your prediction correct?

MULTIPLE IMAGES

Find two good-sized mirrors that are not framed. Set the mirrors at right angles to one another as shown in Figure 18A. To be sure the mirrors are at 90 degrees, look at the image of your face in the mirrors at the place where the mirrors meet.

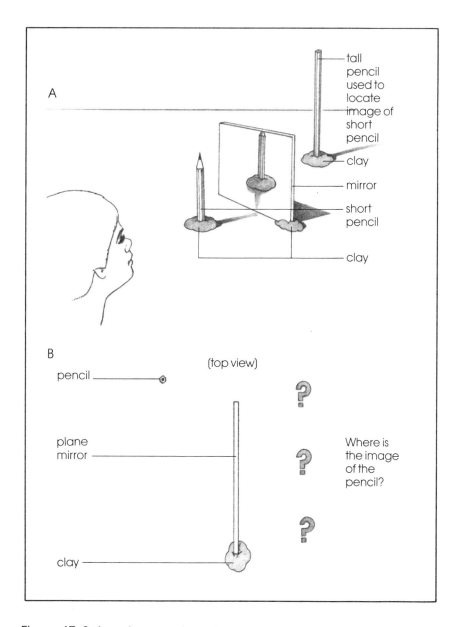

A

tall pencil used to locate image of short pencil

clay

mirror

short pencil

clay

B

pencil

(top view)

plane mirror

Where is the image of the pencil?

clay

Figure 17. Setups for experimenting with mirror images

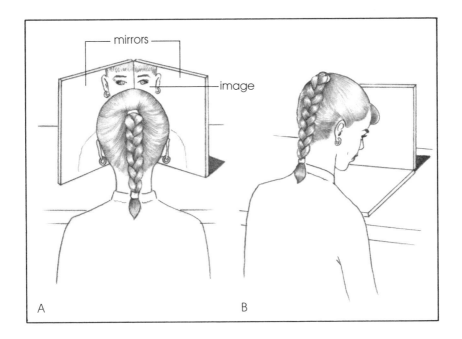

Figure 18. Studying double images

Turn the mirrors until you see a complete, undistorted image of your face.

Once you have adjusted the mirrors, look carefully at your own image. Wink your right eye. Which eye does your image wink? Which eye does your image wink when you look into a single mirror? Turn the two mirrors so they are as shown in Figure 18B. What do you notice about the image of your face now?

Place a small lump of clay between the mirrors as they were in Figure 18A. Stick a short pencil in the clay. Attach a short piece of tape to the right side of the pencil. In this way you'll be able to distinguish between the right and left sides of the pencil. How many images of the pencil do you see when the mirrors are at 90 degrees to one another?

What happens to the number of images as you reduce the angle between the mirrors? Does the number of images change suddenly at certain angles, or is there a gradual increase, say, one for every degree?

Why do you think there are so many images of the toothpick when the mirrors are parallel to each other?

BENDING LIGHT

Light usually travels in straight lines. Of course, it's bent sharply when it is reflected by a mirror. Can light be bent in other ways?

Hold a clear jar full of water on a sheet of light-colored cardboard. Turn the jar and cardboard so that light coming from the sun or a strong light bulb strikes the side of the jar as shown in Figure 19A. Notice how the light is brought to a point by the water. Hold the cardboard sheet parallel to the jar and move it closer to and farther from the jar. You'll find a place where you can see a line of bright light as shown in Figure 19B. Light coming through the jar is bent by the water and brought together at this line.

• If you have a small hand lens, you might like to repeat this experiment using the lens. Can you find a line of light with the lens? Can you make a point of light with the lens? Can you bend light, using your lens, to make upside-down images of lamp bulbs and other objects such as trees that you can see through a window?

• Put some water in a plastic sandwich bag. You can make some lenslike images if you stand back away from a window and hold the bag of water close to a light-colored wall. Light passing through the window and water "lens" will come to focus on the wall where you'll see fuzzy images. By carefully shaping the bag, you can improve the quality of the images.

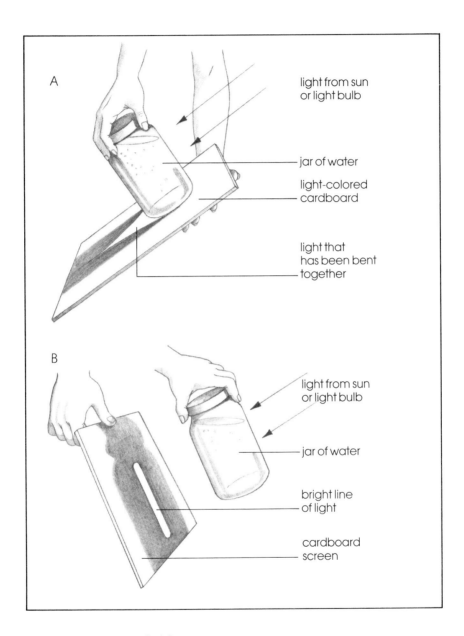

Figure 19. Bending light

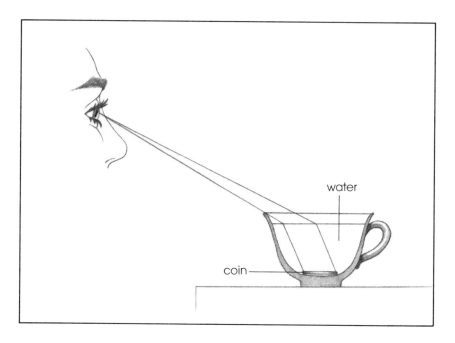

Figure 20. Making a coin appear

• Put a ruler or pencil in a wide drinking glass that is filled with water. Look at the ruler or pencil from above at an angle. Notice how the object appears to bend sharply at the point where it emerges from the water. Of course, it's the light, not the object that's bending.

• Place a coin on the bottom of a teacup. Lower your head until the penny is just hidden from view by the top of the teacup. Now have someone slowly pour water into the cup without disturbing the coin. The coin becomes visible again as the water level rises. Light coming from the coin through the water will bend as it leaves the water and come to your eye as shown in Figure 20.

BOOKS FOR FURTHER READING

Ardley, Neil. *Working with Water.* New York: Watts, 1983.

Attonito, Joan K. *A Science Lab.* Buffalo: DOK, 1982.

Cobb, Vicki. *Science Experiments You Can Eat.* New York: Harper & Row, 1972.

_____. *More Science Experiments You Can Eat.* New York: Harper & Row, 1979.

Gardner, Robert. *Kitchen Chemistry.* New York: Messner, 1982.

_____. *Science Around the House.* New York: Messner, 1985.

_____. *Space: Frontier of the Future.* New York: Doubleday, 1980.

Guide to Animal Tracks. Harrisburg, Pa.: Stackpole, 1976.

Henbest, Nigel, and Couper, Heather. *Physics.* New York: Watts, 1983.

Herbert, Don. *Mister Wizard's Experiments for Young Scientists.* New York: Doubleday, 1959.

_____. *Mister Wizard's Supermarket Science.* New York: Random House, 1980.

Herbert, Don, and Ruchlis, Hy. *Mister Wizard's Four Hundred Experiments in Science.* New York: Book-Lab, 1983.

Johnson, May. *Chemistry Experiments.* Tulsa: EDC Publishing, 1983.

Leon, George deLucenay. *The Electricity Story.* New York: Arco, 1983.

Mandell, Muriel. *Two Hundred & Twenty Easy-to-Do Science Experiments for Young People: Three Complete Books.* New York: Dover, 1985.

Meyer, Jerome S. *Boiling Water in a Paper Cup: And Other Unbelievables.* New York: Scholastic, 1970.

Morgan, Alfred. *Adventures in Electrochemistry.* New York: Scribner's, 1977.

Olaus, Murie J. *A Field Guide to Animal Tracks.* 2d ed. Boston: Houghton Mifflin, 1975.

Reuben, Gabriel. *Electricity Experiments for Children.* New York: Dover, 1960.

Stone, George K. *More Science Projects You Can Do.* Englewood Cliffs, N.J.: Prentice-Hall, 1981.

Walters, Derek. *Chemistry.* New York: Watts, 1983.

Webster, David. *How to Do a Science Project.* New York: Watts, 1974.

Zubrowski, Bernie. *Messing Around with Baking Chemistry.* Boston: Little, Brown, 1981.

_____. *Messing Around with Water Pumps and Siphons.* Boston: Little, Brown, 1981.

INDEX